SandCastle

Keeping the Peace

Learning about Differences

Pam Scheunemann

Consulting Editor, Diane Craig, M.A./Reading Specialist

ABDO
Publishing Company

Published by ABDO Publishing Company, 4940 Viking Drive, Edina, Minnesota 55435.

Copyright © 2004 by Abdo Consulting Group, Inc. International copyrights reserved in all countries. No part of this book may be reproduced in any form without written permission from the publisher. SandCastle™ is a trademark and logo of ABDO Publishing Company.

Printed in the United States.

Credits
Edited by: Pam Price
Curriculum Coordinator: Nancy Tuminelly
Cover and Interior Design and Production: Mighty Media
Photo Credits: BananaStock Ltd., Brand X Pictures, Digital Vision, ImageState, PhotoDisc

Library of Congress Cataloging-in-Publication Data

Scheunemann, Pam, 1955-
    Learning about differences / Pam Scheunemann.
        p. cm. -- (Keeping the peace)
    Includes index.
    Summary: An introduction to the differences in people and how understanding can help foster peace.
    ISBN 1-59197-561-1
    1. Conduct of life--Juvenile literature. 2. Peace--Juvenile literature. 3. Difference (Psychology)--Juvenile literature. [1. Toleration. 2. Prejudices. 3. Interpersonal relations. 4. Peace.] I. Title.

BJ1631.S27 2004
303.6'9--dc22

2003057787

SandCastle™ books are created by a professional team of educators, reading specialists, and content developers around five essential components that include phonemic awareness, phonics, vocabulary, text comprehension, and fluency. All books are written, reviewed, and leveled for guided reading, early intervention reading, and Accelerated Reader® programs and designed for use in shared, guided, and independent reading and writing activities to support a balanced approach to literacy instruction.

Let Us Know

After reading the book, SandCastle would like you to tell us your stories about reading. What is your favorite page? Was there something hard that you needed help with? Share the ups and downs of learning to read. We want to hear from you! To get posted on the ABDO Publishing Company Web site, send us e-mail at:

sandcastle@abdopub.com

SandCastle Level: Transitional

Taking the time
to learn about
others keeps the
peace.

Max, Rita, and Lori met in school and became good friends.

The more you know about others, the better you can understand them.

Jane's skin is a different color than Miki's.

Miki and Jane get to know each other and become best friends.

Todd's friend Carlos is from Spain.

Todd enjoys making a new friend from a different country.

Families are all different.

Jake lives with his dad.

His friend Nick lives with his mom and grandma.

People speak many different languages.

Rosa speaks Spanish and English.

Different countries celebrate different holidays.

In the United States, Marcus celebrates Independence Day with his family.

People have different religious holidays.

Ned is Jewish and celebrates Hanukkah.

Some people have physical disabilities.

Allen is blind.

He uses a white cane to guide him as he walks.

Everyone has different interests.

Ryan likes to play chess.

It's fun to learn about things other people do.

What can you do
to keep the peace?

Glossary

celebrate. to honor with special ceremonies or festivities

different. not alike

family. a group of people related to one another

religious. of or relating to a religion

understand. to know well due to close contact and experience

About SandCastle™

A professional team of educators, reading specialists, and content developers created the SandCastle™ series to support young readers as they develop reading skills and strategies and increase their general knowledge. The SandCastle™ series has four levels that correspond to early literacy development in young children. The levels are provided to help teachers and parents select the appropriate books for young readers.

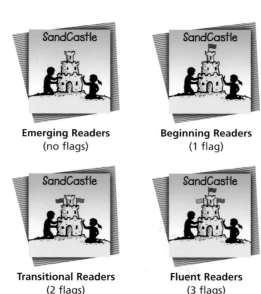

Emerging Readers
(no flags)

Beginning Readers
(1 flag)

Transitional Readers
(2 flags)

Fluent Readers
(3 flags)

These levels are meant only as a guide. All levels are subject to change.

To see a complete list of SandCastle™ books and other nonfiction titles from ABDO Publishing Company, visit **www.abdopub.com** or contact us at:

4940 Viking Drive, Edina, Minnesota 55435 • 1-800-800-1312 • fax: 1-952-831-1632